Introduction to Dish & Bot Beginners

CW00469714

Dueep Jyot Singh

Gardening Series

Mendon Cottage Books

JD-Biz Publishing

All Rights Reserved.

No part of this publication may be reproduced in any form or by any means, including scanning, photocopying, or otherwise without prior written permission from JD-Biz Corp Copyright © 2019

All Images Licensed by Fotolia, Pixabay, and 123RF.

Disclaimer

The information is this book is provided for informational purposes only. The information is believed to be accurate as presented based on research by the author.

The author or publisher is not responsible for the use or safety of any procedure or treatment mentioned in this book. The author or publisher is not responsible for errors or omissions that may exist.

Our books are available at

1. Amazon.com

2. Barnes and Noble

3. Itunes

4. Kobo

5. Smashwords

6. Google Play Books

Download Free Books!

http://MendonCottageBooks.com

Table of Contents

Introduction

A couple of decades ago I saw a friend picking up a large glass carboys, in which chemical liquids had been transported, from outside a manufacturing unit, and when I wanted to know what she would do with that container, she said – can you think of a better container in which to make a miniature garden?

At that time I had not even thought of the beauty of a miniature garden, in your interior, as a part of the design of your living room. That was because I was so used, to living in places where I had huge outdoor gardens, so bringing in the plants indoors was not something of which I had thought!

Later on, living in cities, and apartments, where the nearest outdoor garden was 25 stories below, and just one tiny patch of green, in a concrete jungle, I began to think that yes miniature gardens was one of the best ways in which I could bring a bit of greenery right inside my limited pigeonholed letterbox of a living space.

It does not matter how large or small, your container is, as long as they are waterproof and attractive. The glass also has to be transparent, so that you can see your plants clearly and the sun and light can pass through the glass on your plants. I have seen bottle gardens made in French glass storage bottles of 6.6 gallons called bonbonnes. These were used, to store small quantities of wines.

If you have the time and the energy, you could go around shops dealing in secondhand goods, and you might find these vintage bonbonnes there, especially if you are in a wine growing area, in America they are called demijohns and the capacity may vary.

Do not ever make your miniature garden in plastic carboys even though they are so commonly available all over the place. Any plant in a plastic container with the sun shining on it is going to suffer terribly because of the heat. Besides, I really do not find plastic containers to be aesthetically pleasing, in indoor gardens. There is absolutely nothing natural in them, nor are they eco-friendly.

For making your miniature garden, it is not necessary that you just bother about bottles as containers. If you have an aquarium which you have not been using for a long time, this is also going to be a really beautiful garden receptacle. The nicest thing about an aquarium is that the top is so wide, that you do not have to use bamboo sticks in order to manipulate your plants, through a narrow hole, which may possibly be the case in your demijohns or in your carboys.

The making of such a garden is going to take some patience and some skill, but as it is a very fascinating and intriguing hobby, especially for first-time gardeners, you might find yourself so fascinated with the results that you may go around the neighborhood looking for glass containers, in which to plant future gardens. Who knows, this may not only be the beginning of a brand-new friendship, but also the beginning offer prosperous small home business!

Overfilled bottle garden!

You can fill an empty corner of your room with these bottle gardens and make them more attractive and less boring. You can also stand them on a table. Or if you want to be the really dramatic sauce, and you have a Hollywood type of staircase going up, you can stand your body garden at the head of the stairs, so that Clark Gable going up can have an enjoyable view of the details as he mounts the stairs, à la Gone with the Wind.

The creativity and imagination, which can be utilized in the making of a bottle garden, is going to depend on you. I have seen bottle gardens with pools, – made of little round pieces of mirror – paths made of pebbles, lawns made of mosses, little huts and houses and even bridges. When you are making a bottle garden with just a given number of plants, do not mix succulents and cacti with them. That is because succulents and cacti the last water, but you are making a mini rainforest and ecosystem in your bottle garden, if you cork it. The greenhouse effect is going to keep your bottle garden well watered, through water evaporation. And condensation. But your cacti and succulents would not like that sort of hothouse atmosphere with "rain" dripping over them every afternoon whenever the sun shines into the glass, especially if it has been placed on your windowsill.

A 'Terrarium' Is Not A Bottle Garden

I would like to make one thing clear here. All over the Internet, the word terrarium is being used as a term to explain a bottle garden. A terrarium is not a bottle garden. So any sort of gardener with plenty of interesting content on the internet tells me that she is or he is going to give me tips to make a really interesting terrarium, the first thing I am going to ask her, all right, where do I get the lizards, snakes, and other reptiles or amphibians, which can be placed in their terrarium.

This is almost as bad as picking up a tiny miniature dwarf variety plant, and then telling you to admire my bonsai. So if you are looking for information on how to make bottle gardens online, and they tell you that to put the soil in the terrarium, you need such and such equipment, go to another site, where they tell you, to put the soil in your bottle garden, you need such and such equipment. At least this person knows of what he speaks, and he is using the proper gardening term.

The knowledgeable and experienced zoologist knows what a terrarium or a vivarium or a riparium is. But that particular zoological term terrarium being grabbed by ignorant gardeners to explain a bottle garden is misleading, false, and ill-informed. On the Internet, they tell you that a terrarium is a place in which you can monitor the growth of plants, as written on Wikipedia. But as any knowledgeable person knows that Wikipedia is the greatest purveyor of misleading and wrong information on the Internet, anything written there is going to be cut copy pasted on a large number of sites and considered to be the truth, and nothing but the truth.

When I told my friend, that a terrarium is not a bottle garden, she told me that she had read it in a gardening book. And it was everywhere on the Internet. And I had better get my facts straight. She was telling a botanist this, with University Science Degrees in zoology and botany! The word was synonymous with a miniature garden or an indoor garden in a bottle. Interesting, because this word has come into Vogue, only in the 20th century, when in the days long past, scientific observation bottles ending in – ium did not mean greenhouse gardens.

Well, that supposed gardener may have written a very fascinating book on gardening, but just this word terrarium being misused canceled out all his knowledge and credibility.

Dish Gardens and Trough Gardens

Apart from bottle gardens, dish gardens and trough gardens are also fascinating methods with which you can grow your plants indoors, as long as the troughs are not made up of plastic or metal. Like I said, you may think that they are easily available, but they are not aesthetically pleasing. Any dishes and troughs made of porcelain, glass, or any other such traditional materials including clay – not concrete – can be used for making dish gardens and trough gardens.

The choice of plants that you are going to be planting in your miniature garden is very important. They have to be botanically related enough to be able to bear the same sort of living and growing conditions. That is why I advised you before hand not to put succulents and cacti with rainforest plants, and vice versa.

For an aesthetically pleasing garden, your selection should have a large number of plants of different heights. Difference in color and foliage is also going to add attraction to your plant collection. One tall one is going to be the leader. Surrounding it are going to be a large number of bushy contrasting plants as a foil and a contrast. Also they should not be so overpowering that some plants decide to overrun their neighbors and take over your little miniature garden. That is why you are not going to plant mint here! But a couple of trailers, if you are growing your garden in a large container can be draped artistically over your tall plant. These are best suitable for your trough or your dish garden, because they can overhang from the sides, gracefully.

A number of containers and troughs are easily available for your trough or dish garden. Just go around junk shops and antique shops and be on the lookout for pretty vintage pieces, keeping into view how much you want to spend on them – unless they are so beautiful that you consider it really worth it, going overboard with your budget, after all, you have to look at them for the next 50 years or so every day – in fact a vintage soup tureen is ideal for starters. You can also look for porcelain basins, used for washing hands and faces, in the Victorian times. Some of them are really beautiful, especially if they have designs drawn on them, before they were put into the oven for firing and glazing.

Copper preserving pans were very much in vogue in every kitchen, about 200 ago, and you find them very rarely today. Our great-grandmothers called them jam pans.

Not many of us have the time, inclination, energy, or even wish to slave over a hot kitchen, making preserves in this pan. But it can be beautifully utilized in the making of a garden. Latter-day nurseries can provide you with troughs made of wood, conical baskets, clay dishes, and also some fancy ones made of wrought-iron.

Making your own garden with your own choice of plants is a much better option than going online, looking at something fascinating, paying all use some of money, and wondering when it is going to reach you, if ever. This happened with one of my relatives in SF, especially when she did not bother to check out the credentials of that supposed online nursery, which was a fly-by-night operator, selling you bonsais, plant seedlings, seeds, miniature gardens, bottle gardens and so on. And one wonders how many people paid for the photographs online, which were so fascinating and bewitching.

There are 2 ways in which you can make a dish garden or a trough garden. The first one is taking potted plants, already planted in their containers or in their faults, and remove them from their original containers. Then you plant them in their new trough container, with a number of other plants. So you have a grouping of plants with a similar growing condition characteristic.

Naturally, you need to have good drainage. The other method is put a layer of moist garden compost or peat in a container, in which you are going to stand a large number of smaller pots, in which plants are already growing. These plants are not going to be removed from their containers. You are now going to pack the outside of the containers to the rim with peat.

Again, remember that these plants are **not** going to have different, assorted and various environmental conditions, even though they may be growing in diverse and dissimilar types of soil. That means the levels of watering are going to be different. However, you can plant a number of bulbs and flowering plants in these potted plant troughs, or dish gardens so that it does not matter which time of the year it is. There is always going to be something blooming in your garden, indoors, all year around.

Also, if you are planting potted plants in your dish or trough garden, you can always hide the rims of the containers with pebbles, moss, driftwood, stones or whatever else you wish.

Miniature gardens, especially those made in a bottle are a bit more complicated, when you are making them, because you may want to include extra features in them to make them more attractive. Like pools, paths, and anything extra, but even though a little bit of designing is needed, you are going to plan them the same way; you made your dish garden.

Do not worry about plant combinations. If you know that one particular plant which you wanted to incorporate in your miniature garden does not suit the environmental characteristics of your other choice of plants, there are plenty of other choices and combinations available out there. You have the whole world from which to choose, as long as they grow along with your original plant choices, as well as in your region. But the advantage of bottle gardens is that you do not have to bother about harsh weather outside. They are already in their own limited ecosystem and protective container. So you can be a little bit adventurous.

Preparing Your Bottle Garden

A squeaky clean bottle is a joy forever. Instead of using dishwashing solution and a brush, use crushed abrasive eggshells, 3 tablespoons full in one liter bottles, fill the bottle up with water, cap it and shake shake shake, until all the deposit by the sides of the bottles is removed with the gentle abrasion. No poisonous chemicals used. And if you do not have a bottle brush, they did not have them around, very often, 2 centuries ago, when they were using these abrasive materials with which to clean the insides of bottles, apart from bicarbonate of soda and salt, and boiling water.

A large sized bottle with a wide neck is always preferable, because you can put your hand in easily. White glass is preferable, even though colored glasses are suitable as long as they are not deep in color and prevent you from watching the growth of your plants from outside.

You can also use a 12 inch or a 10 inch diameter bowl, with a lid, which is airtight. Take a goldfish bowl on which you can fit an suitable airtight lid. Once you plant your plants, such an airtight container, even delicate plants which need warmth, no drafts and a moist atmosphere are going to flourish.

That is why a goldfish bowl is going to be more suitable and easily manageable, than a narrow necked carboy.

After you have washed your container and dried it thoroughly, so that no vestiges of moisture remain, – leave it to dry on a sunny sill – which means that all the cells that you are going to put in is going to stick to the walls of the container.

The soil is going to consist of sand and organic humus. A mixture of these 2 items are going to be the growing material in your bottle, and I will show you how to do the planting later. But it is a narrow necked carboys or a bottle of your choice, use a funnel and pour a layer of sand about 3 cm as your bottom most layer. As you are not going to knock a hole into your precious carboys, so that the water can drain away, this sand is going to be your drainage system. The environment is going to be confined. It is also going to be humid. So adequate drainage is necessary, and also a medium for the absorption of the water droplets.

What You Are *Not* Going to Put in Your Bottle

There are some plants, which you are going to avoid as assiduously as possible. These include plants that flower, in your narrow necked carboy, which you are going to close with an airtight container. Flowering plants, after they have flowered are going to fall on the floor of the bottle, when their day is done. And then they are going to rot in the moisture of the soil surface.

Any green plant, which grows rapidly and vigorously and takes over all the area, avoid like the plague. The same thing goes for cacti as I said before, they do not enjoy a humid and muggy atmosphere.

Green plants, which are small and which can be placed easily into the bottle can be chosen as long as you know that they are not going to grow up into large oaks, from little acorns.

Here is one tip for your garden. You may find green spots occurring upon your glass walls, which is algal growth and which is not a fungal mold. They like muggy atmospheres, which allow them to proliferate really quickly. Do not use any chemical product, especially dishwasher liquid or car window cleaner with which to clean your glass bottle surface! You want to poison your plants with chemicals? Just take a piece of sponge which you have attached to a wooden rod/rigid wire or bamboo chopstick, which can enter your carboy and can be manipulated easily. Scrub the sides with this cleaner, which is the sponge dipped in a decoction made up of 5 cloves of garlic in a little bit of water, allowed to boil and steep for about 20 minutes. Best antiseptic cleanser and remover of those green spots.

If you find water droplets forming on the sides and the walls of your bottle, what do you do? You want to see your plants clearly, but you could do without the fog. The reason why this fog has been caused is because of the difference in heat between the outside atmosphere, in the room and the temperature inside your carboys. It is hot in your room, but it is cool in the carboys. I am using the word carboys here, but you can understand it to be an aquarium, a bottle, or any container.

So move your carboys immediately away from the source of heat, so that the water droplets can trickle-down and get absorbed into the soil.

Best Plants Choices

I would of course like plants which are tiny, attractive, about 4 to 10 cm in height or depending.

So you can begin with the Begonia family – boweri and rotundifolia.

Cryptanthus Acaulis Variegata – native to Brazil, but very attractive, and members of this family are called the Star family because of their shape. This particular variety is known as the earth Star.

Episcia genus different varieties – they are creeping plants, with white and orange red flowers, and green foliage.

Fittonia verschaffeltii – another creeping plant with little yellow colored flowers, and a bronze foliage.

Euonymus japonicus "Microphyllus Variegatus" – best choice of shrubs you want in your bottle garden, it is just 30 cm in height. Flowers are greenish white. Foliage is dark green and edged in white.

Pellaea rotundifolia – this is a fern up to 10 cm in height with foliage which is dark green in color.

Ficus pumila – as a contrast in foliage, this has a lighter colored foliage. And as it is a creeping plant, you can consider it the right choice to cover the bottom of your bottle's surface and an adequate foil for the rest of the plants.

Pilea cadierei "Minima, Fittonia verschaffeltii, Sansevieria hahnii, Maranta leuconeura, Peliionia daveauana are some popular and common choices, which can be also used as starters. With so many plant choices all over the world, and so many species from which to choose, especially those who have very small dwarf varieties growing naturally, making a choice is not difficult at all.

Equipment for Your Miniature Garden

You do not have to spend lots and lots of money on equipment as long as you have a spoon, which you can use as a shovel, some bamboo chopsticks for digging holes in the sand, a fork, which is going to be your rake as well as gardening fork, and for ramming and fixing the plants to the soil, after you have planted them in the holes dug for them, just take a cotton reel.

Smear enough of adhesive on one side of a bamboo chopstick. Now stick it in through the cotton reel's hole, so that the joint is secure and fixed. This is a good way in which you can tamp down the soil, after the planting is done so that the plant is fixed properly into its soil base and the roots can adhere to the soil.

For removing any dead leaves or dying flowers, just use tweezers or small tongs, if the container is larger. If you do not have these, just sharpen one end of the bamboo chopstick, and use it for spearing those leaves and flowers and pulling them out of the neck of the bottle.

Apart from sand, you also need to place a layer of broken pottery and pebbles, for drainage. Now place the organic potting compost on top of this layer. You can also make the design slanting and undulating by using your fork from the back to the front over the compost, if you have made a little mountain in one corner. Creativity is all

Consolidate all the compost with the help of your rammer by tamping it down.

After that, take all the selected plants and arrange them in such a manner, in a bowl full of compost, with the surface area about as much as that in these file of the bottle garden. This is how you are going to look at the design before hand and arrange it to your own satisfaction.

Cryptanthus being added with the help of tweezers into the bottle. You can also see some moss and some pieces of driftwood already inserted into the bottle. Like I said, creativity is everything, with whatever you have. Just make a hole in the compost, and then maneuver the plant of your choice into the hole, with the pair of tweezers or with the chopsticks. A little bit of manual dexterity will be needed here.

I saw some really experienced gardeners doing this really well, in a 1965 documentary, made by Pathe, when bottle gardens were coming into vogue and existence. You can see that documentary just for fun, in the conclusion section.

My choice of creeper – Ficus pumila. Position it where you want, before tamping it down with your hammer.

Selaginella – fern is extremely pretty, so just take a few of these pieces and add them into your bottle.

You are now going to cover the roots with the soil and tamp them firmly with your rammer. Your main aim is to make sure that your plants do not move around just because they have not been firmly fixed into the soil.

With the addition of the fern, you have begun to get a feel of the rainforest, along with the moss. And because the compost has been made of humus and natural organic material, it looks like a natural

ecosystem. You can also add some stones and pebbles, like I said, creativity is all.

Start planting from the outside, and begin moving towards the inside. Also make sure that the plant leaves or any portions of the plant do not get squashed against the walls of the container because each part of the plant has to be free to grow, even if it is in a contained atmosphere of a bottle.

Adding some earthworms is going to add value to your bottle.

Do some watering by using distilled water with a spray.

If any sort of condensation begins to form by the sides of the glass, that means the glass has been kept in the sun for a longish while and has heated up. So place your miniature Garden in a place away from the sun, so that the gentle rain can shower upon your plants. But you need to see some sort of condensation, in the morning and in the evening so that you know that there is enough of moisture in the bottle to permit photosynthesis – manufacture of food with the help of sunlight.

After you have done the watering, you will need to dry the inside of the bottle, so that it does not fog up, when you cork the bottle. You can use a piece of sponge attached on a piece of wire to remove the last traces of water and the soil from the inside of the glass.

When watering the plants with this spray apparatus, look for a small one, with a nozzle which is set at some sort of angle which can be inserted inside the narrow neck of the carboy.

If you want, you can use a cork to make the mouth of the bottle airtight. There you are, you have a complete ecosystem and this bottle is going to last on forever and forever.

If you want, you can go into the garden and look for some critters under some pieces of wood or rocks. If you are not afraid of them, you just pick them up in your shovel and bring them in. This is going to add a new dimension to your green house ecosystem.

After you have closed the top of the bottle, it is going to steam up, within a couple of hours. That means the photosynthesis system has begun to work, and your ecosystem is now completely functional. You do not need to water your bottle garden again, for the next two months, depending on the amount of water which was added to the soil, when you first planted the plants. However, you need to watch it carefully to make sure that it does not dry up or dry out. That means the watering amount was not adequate in the first place. Or maybe you have put it directly into the sun, and the direct rays of the sun beating every day through the glass is heating it up, and getting rid of the moisture in the soil and in your natural ecosystem.

Many people have made these bottle gardens and forgotten about watering them, for the next 50 years. That is because the soil was nutritious, with rich humus. There can also be some insect life added to your miniature Garden. Earthworms, critters from your garden, called springtails or Collembola, just imagine that you are walking in a rain forest, and the floor of the forest is teeming with insect life. If they have been flourishing for millenniums in nature, they are going to flourish in your bottle garden, as long as they are not pests.

Do not collect centipedes, because their stings are venomous. Do not add any slugs either! Nevertheless, I would suggest staying with earthworms, because they are universally beloved and well-known and easily recognizable as the gardener's best friends!

Trying Your Hand at a Moss Garden

This is an activity which children are going to love to do, especially when they see the moss growing right in front of them, on a dish. Moss is a very soft, green and absorbent plant, which grows as a mossy carpet or a cushion, in an area, which is full of moisture. Along with lichens, you are going to see mosses growing by the sides of walls, trees, and even rocks, where they have plenty of access to water in a moist atmosphere.

When I was growing up in mountainous regions, where it rained 300 days out of 365, it was natural that we were very used to ferns, mosses, lichens, algae, and other plants belonging to the bryophyte and pteridophyte genus, species and families, growing in gay profusion and surrounding us wherever we went, very young. Also, our curriculum had begun teaching us plant classification and taxonomy, from class Vth onwards. No wonder many of us grew up to become botany teachers!

The moss plant is flowerless because it is one of the most primitive of plants, existing on earth, much before flowering plants came into existence, and they propagated themselves through spores.

These spores grow in brown capsules which are found at the end of stalks.

Each tiny individual plant is going to go into the making of a thick layer and carpet, depending on the amount of water available and moisture in the atmosphere.

Moss needs lots of water, so when you are making a Moss garden, go Moss hunting in the winter, if the world around you has not been covered with snow and harsh winds blowing all over the area to make one feel rather miserable, especially if one is a sun worshiper.

But this is the time, especially midwinter, when mosses grow prolifically in the woods, and they are at their best. But that is only when you are living in an atmosphere full of water and moisture. Do a little bit of digging of all kinds of moss varieties that you can see, especially on a wintry morning which is pleasant and mild.

Arrange all your moss in a flat layer, over a flat clay dish or a clay tray, which you have filled up with compost beforehand and watered so that it is not dry, when you are doing the planting.

The moss that you have collected is going to come away with some natural material, which allowed it to adhere to the tree bark surface, or to the wall surface. Do not get rid of this material, – [by pulling it away, or putting the moss into water, in the hope of removing it because it is so Brown, flaky, crumbly, whatever, newbie botanists collecting plants from the outdoors. Do this mistake, because they are under the impression that a plant has to be washed free of adhering soil and humus before it is planted anywhere else, Big Mistake Number One of gardening] – because this is the compost, in which the moss roots are embedded.

Add some local ferns, depending on your location, to add variety and color to your Moss garden. The little twigs are a creative little bridge in this little moss forest!

Make sure that all the mosses are contained within your container and do not straggle over the edges. If that happens, this mosses going to act as a siphon. That is going to dry out your garden. Like I said, mosses love plenty of moisture, so make sure that it is well sprayed once a week, so that it does not dry out and grow all brown. If the weather is hot and the humidity level is low, water your Moss garden more often.

A spray shower is best, because it is almost just like the rainfall in the normal natural atmosphere of the moss's natural habitat. If you want to add a little bit more of color and variety to your moss garden, you can plants pretty little flowers like pansies or any other flowers of your choice or if you have a really good selection of moss, with different moss varieties in your garden, you can keep it entirely mossy.

Making Your Succulent and Cactus Garden in a Dish

A number of succulents and cactus plants planted in a dish is always going to be an attractive addition to your indoor garden or even outside on your balcony or patio.

Another interesting variation of your bottle garden plants is choosing a number of succulents, especially when you have so many fascinating and diverse varieties from which to choose. The best thing about succulents are that they do not need enough of water, they are so different, and for all those people, who are under the impression that cacti are boring, thorny plants, they have never seen different cacti in full bloom!

So if you have an inclination to express your artistic and creative taste, and have a large number of succulents floating around, do not bother about searching for containers in which to plant them, just pick up a tray, or dish.

Fill the bottom layer with organic material, humus, stones, pebbles, for drainage, if there are no holes punched into the tray. You can also cover the bottom layer of your container/dish/tray with broken pieces of brick or crocks for proper drainage.

There are so many creative layouts, which you can think, when you are making a dish garden, which any sort of arrangement or design detail here is going to be so much of my idea, without you using your own ideas!

So if you follow these general principles, which we have implemented in the making of bottle gardens, success is going to be certain. The artistic effect is naturally going to depend on the materials you have at hand, and how creative you want to be.

As long as the arrangement between the rocks and the plants and perhaps little pieces of twigs and sticks to make up a scene really are a landscape are harmonious and appealing to the eye at first sight, there is no limits to your imagination.

For containers, you can use bowls of any size and shape. They can be without or with drainage, because even though succulent plants do not need plenty of water, any amount of water which has been left stagnating for a large amount of time in a succulent container is going to rot the roots as well as cause soil to become sour.

When you are watering succulents, you have to make sure, like you do any other plant, that all the water is being absorbed by the soil and it is not over watered.

Not very showy pieces of ceramic pottery as well as neutral colored bowls are a good choice with which to start. That is because if your succulents are very colorful, and your cacti are blooming in different colors and the pot is made up of clashing colors, one is going to blink, literally and figuratively speaking.

The organic soil has a sprinkling of white aquarium gravel in it, just to make it look pretty. It is not perlite or vermiculite. I do not like this latest gardening fad anywhere near my garden, nor do I advocate it to gardeners looking for parting organic soil, bought from their nearest nursery.

The best compost for your succulents is going to be made up of sand and organic humus, in whatever proportions you want. Seriously speaking, everybody has his own idea about proportions and the discussion is equal into World War III. But then, use your own logic. If the succulent has been growing in a desert area, with just a bare minimum of nutrients, bare minimum of water, and in a sandy ground, how do you expect it to live in clay soil or soil which becomes waterlogged very easily because of water retention?

As for perlite and vermiculite – think of that volcanic stone, thrown up during volcanic eruptions. Think of that dust and powder going into your lungs. This is what vermiculite and perlite is made up of. And you are using it in your garden, I have seen gardeners on gardening sites on the Internet and even in nurseries with their faces covered with a thin facemask, busy sifting this material into their pots.

Somebody told them that it was dangerous for their lungs and respiratory system. So they put on a facemask and went on right ahead, sifting the powder into their pots. No comment. Also, common sense is not so common.

Like I said, the selection of the plants and the placement depends entirely on you, and on the availability of the plants that you have ready at hand.

If you want, you can cover the surface with aquarium gravel. It is quite pretty. It is not perlite and vermiculite. You do not want to poison your fishes in your aquarium with this material, do you? But you do not mind inhaling it because somebody told you that this is the best potting compost recommended by some gardening group or guru many light-years away. You can also add some rock crystals or anything you like to give the finishing touches to your cacti garden.

If you want, you can also add colorful chippings, sand, and whatever else you want, on top of the gravel instead of aquarium gravel. If your bowl has holes for drainage, remember to cover this with a broken piece of clay flowerpot, arcwise over the hole so that water can drain away, and the rest can be absorbed in the clay and the soil.

You may perhaps want to add a little bit of charcoal, which they have been doing for centuries to keep the soil sweet. I do that, with powdered charcoal, to all my pots and containers. Thanks to this charcoal, you are not going to have a sour soil with any sort of green growth, just because the water has not drained away properly.

You can also add sandstones, limestone, and small rock structures in order to make this a desert landscape, and for a more pleasing aesthetic effect.

To make a small hillside in your scene, place a large piece of rock at the base of the incline of your pile of rock and compost. This will look like a substantial and heavy foundation.

Succulent plants are not to be watered immediately after you have planted them. We have a tendency to pick up the spray bottle, the moment we have finished planting our plants in any sort of tray, container, pan, box and pot and giving them a thorough dowsing. You do not do that for succulents and cacti.

The watering should be delayed for some days until you know that the plants have "caught" and there is no damage to the roots, especially when the plants have been transplanted from one container to another.

You are not going to use a spray bottle for watering your succulent plants. Repeat, you are NOT going to use spray bottles for spraying your succulents. This means that you are imitating the natural condition of rain in the desert. So what the plant does is grow little tiny roots, to absorb as much of water as it can, while it can. Because, hey, it is raining, and when the spraying is done, after a couple of days, the roots die out, because there is no water.

So be like this intelligent young man, watering his succulent when the soil was completely dry with a long spout watering can.

With this long spout can, he can water around the plants while giving the soil a thorough and complete soaking. Do the watering carefully with no powerful jet coming out to disturb the soil away from the roots.

Your bowl/dish garden should always be placed in the sunniest area, on your windowsill, because succulents love the sun. Unless of course the temperature is in its high 40s, that is when you will need to shift them to the shade. Succulent plants need plenty of light and air. If the place is not lighted properly, the chlorophyll production will not be adequate enough to keep your plant healthy. Light, air and water is necessary for good production and photosynthesis for plants. In the absence of these natural elements your plant is going to starve to death.

Remember to turn your bowl's position every week, so that all the rest of the plants can also get their proper amount of sun, especially when one area may be in the comparative shade, overshadowed by a larger succulent plant during many hours of the day.

If you are using a nonporous bowl, as is so popular nowadays, with all those nonbiodegradable, plasticky, kitschy, wonder-what-material products coming into the market, watering has to be done very carefully. Because, thanks to no pores, the water cannot evaporate, like it would do, through a natural clay surface. So that water stays on in your pot. And if it does not have adequate and proper drainage facilities, well, like I said, root rot is going to set in double quick before you say Jackie Robinson.

Excess water in a pot is going to stagnate unless it has a way of evaporating or getting absorbed by the soil. If you are over watering your succulents and your cactus, which they do not need, but you decided that they must need water, all that extra water is accumulating at the bottom of your bowl and dish. That immediately leads to souring of the soil. That is why for cactuses and succulents, you always have to make sure that the soil is completely dry before you try out any other watering stunt on them. Drying does not mean just the top layer is dry. It means that the soil is dry in the container, through and through, top, middle and bottom layer.

Watering your succulents may be necessary, a bit more in the summer, even though, believe it or not, my mother has not watered her succulents and cacti on her terrace garden for the past eight months. And they are going strong. In winter, I would not suggest doing any sort of watering. If you have kept your cacti dish garden indoors, and the central heating is on, it is going to get as dehydrated as you are getting dehydrated. It has no way of getting a tall drink of water, like you are doing, just because you felt that you needed it. So this is when you will need to water it every three weeks, especially if you have the heat running high in your closed, muggy rooms, every winter, 24/7.

Naturally, you are going to come down with a respiratory infection. That is how people died down the centuries, from TB, because they were under the impression that closed rooms were best places in which to live and fresh air brought with it poisonous miasmas. And we consider ourselves educated and comparatively intelligent and sensible, even though we are doing the same thing to ourselves, with air conditioning and central heating. At least allow your cactus plants to survive in this atmosphere.

Who says cactus plants are bland and boring and not interesting at all?

The best succulents choice belong to the *Opuntia, echinocactus, Ferocactus, Rebutia, Mammillaria, Chamaecereus, Crassula, Aeonium, Echeveria, Delospermia, Sedum ,Haworthia, Senecio etc* families. Their plants are available easily all over the world, no matter what the temperature is like outside, there is going to be a succulent or a cactus, which has managed to adapt itself to the atmosphere and natural conditions of that particular place.

Conclusion

This book has given you information on how you can make up your own bottle garden and dish garden, starting as a hobby and then extending it to a really relaxing activity.

Here is an amusing 1965 documentary made on bottle gardens, on YouTube, by Pathe, where somebody decided that acid carboys could be best utilized in making bottle gardens and then sold for Christmas presents. Naturally, these acid carboys are scrubbed very well to get rid of all chemical traces even though plants do not mind just a little tiny trace of HCl and sulfuric acid.

https://www.youtube.com/watch?v=Vi_tCvarfG0

So what are you waiting for, if you have a large number of plants, which you intended to plant, individually, in their own containers when you prepared them with soil and so on and so forth, ho-hum, it is much better to plant them all in one large container, a bottle garden, or a tray, or a dish or a soup tureen, as long as you have more than 4 inches of soil depth in which the roots can grow. You are not growing bonsais.

Who knows, one fine day your bottle garden may be sold at Christie's, by your future generations for oodles of money. It is quite well known that the acid carboys and demijohns of the 20th century and the 19th century are quite rare vintage pieces today. Also, they are very expensive, when you go to buy them online, the Once upon a time, they were so common, to store wine, that every self-respecting cellar had their glass demijohns in different capacities to hold wine.

Live Long and Prosper!

Author Bio

Dueep Jyot Singh is a Management and Education Professional who managed to gather Postgraduate Degrees in Management and English and Degrees in Science, French and Education while pursuing different enjoyable career options like being IT,SEO and HRD Database Manager/ trainer, movie , radio and TV scriptwriter, theatre artiste and public speaker, lecturer in French, Marketing and Advertising, an hospital administrator, ex-Editor of Hearts On Fire (now known as Solstice) Books Missouri USA, advice columnist and cartoonist, publisher and Aviation School trainer, ex-moderator on Medico.in, banker, student councilor ,travelogue writer … among other things!

One fine morning, she decided that she had enough of killing herself by Degrees and went back to her first love—writing. It's more enjoyable! She already has 48 published academic and 14 fiction- in- different- genre books under her belt.

When she is not designing websites, writing bilingual poetry or translating ancient traditional songs into French and English or making Graphic design illustrations for clients, she is browsing through old bookshops hunting for treasures, of which she has an enviable collection – including R.L. Stevenson, O.Henry, Dornford Yates, Maurice Walsh, De Maupassant, Victor Hugo, Sapper, C.N. Williamson, "Bartimeus" and the crown of her collection- Dickens "The Old Curiosity Shop," and "Martin Chuzzlewit" and so on… Just call her "Renaissance Woman" - collecting herbal remedies, acting like Universal Helping Hand/Agony Aunt, or escaping to her dear mountains for a bit of exploring, collecting herbs and plants, and trekking.

Check out some of the other JD-Biz Publishing books

Gardening Series on Amazon

Download Free Books!

http://MendonCottageBooks.com

Health Learning Series

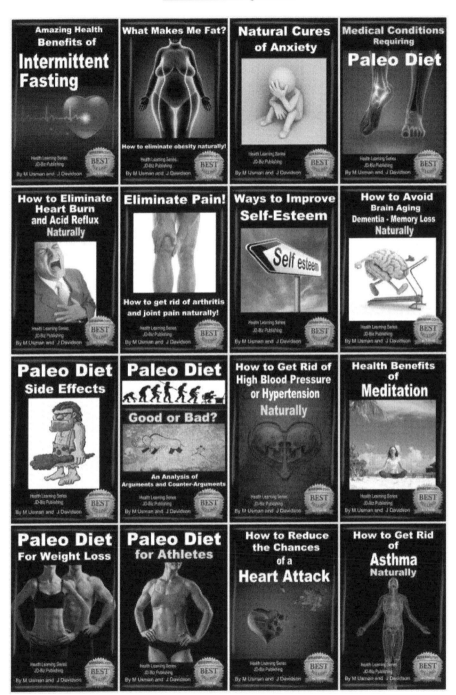

Amazing Animal Book Series

Chinchillas • Beavers • Snakes • Dolphins • Wolves • Walruses

Polar Bears • Turtles • Bees • Frogs • Horses • Monkeys

Dinosaurs • Sharks • Whales • Spiders • Big Cats • Big Mammals of Yellowstone

Animals of Australia • Sasquatch - Yeti Abominable Snowman Bigfoot • Giant Panda Bears • Kittens • Komodo Dragons • Lady Bugs

Animals of North America • Meerkats • Birds of North America • Penguins • Hamsters • Elephants

Learn To Draw Series

How to Build and Plan Books

Entrepreneur Book Series

Our books are available at

1. Amazon.com

2. Barnes and Noble

3. Itunes

4. Kobo

5. Smashwords

6. Google Play Books

Download Free Books!

http://MendonCottageBooks.com

Publisher

JD-Biz Corp

P O Box 374

Mendon, Utah 84325

http://www.jd-biz.com/

Mendon Cottage Books

P O Box 374, Mendon Utah 84325

Printed in Great Britain
by Amazon

58167782R00033